Date Due			

IF YOU WERE AN...

Astronaut

IF YOU WERE AN . . .

Astronaut

Virginia Schomp

BENCHMARK BOOKS

MARSHALL CAVENDISH
NEW YORK

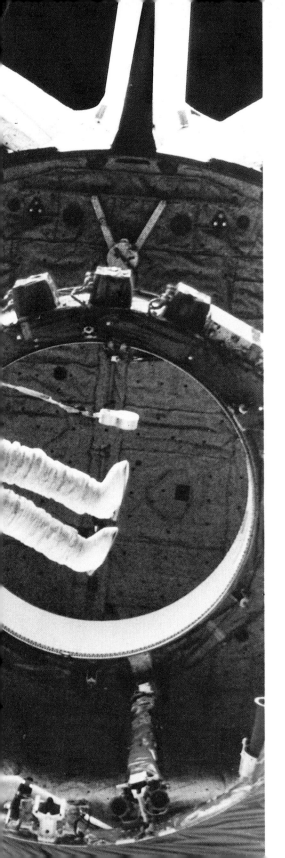

High above Earth, two astronauts take a "walk" outside their spaceship.

If you were an astronaut, you would ride a rocket into space. Through your window, Earth looks like a beautiful blue-green ball.

What will you do so high above home? Will you rescue a lost satellite? Will you help build a floating laboratory for scientists? Maybe you'll set up the first houses on the Moon or take the first step on Mars.

Who knows what adventures you might have sailing among the stars if you were an astronaut!

5

Before you head for the stars, there's lots to find out on Earth. New astronauts go to a training school run by NASA—the National Aeronautics and Space Administration. In school, they learn about the space shuttle, the only spaceship that takes off like a rocket and lands like a plane.

The dials and switches on this simulator are just like the controls in a real space shuttle.

Astronauts must learn how to parachute, in case of emergencies during take-off or landing.

How do astronauts become shuttle experts? They practice on simulators—full-size copies of different parts of the spaceship. Working with these models, students learn to fly and land the shuttle, use the equipment, and protect themselves in emergencies.

Riders on the KC-135 airplane enjoy a quick trip through a world without gravity.

Astronauts also must get used to living and working in space. On Earth, an invisible force called gravity pulls everything toward the ground. In space, there is so little gravity that everything floats. Scientists call this zero-gravity, or zero-G. Astronauts call it fun!

If you were training to be an astronaut, you would learn about zero-G by flying in a special airplane. The plane climbs fast and high. Suddenly it falls. For a minute, all the passengers inside float through the air like feathers in a breeze.

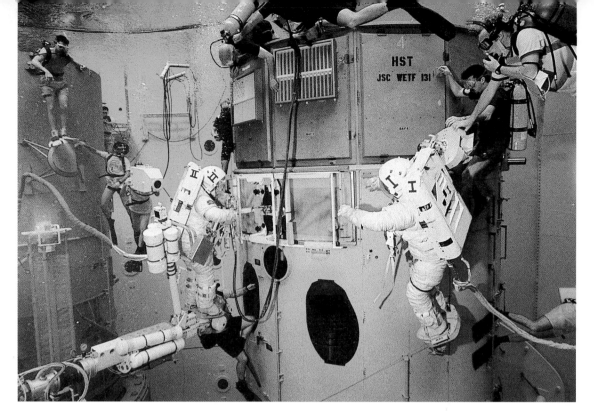

In a deep pool, astronauts practice repairs they will make in space.

After training, astronauts look forward to their turn on a space flight. Flights are called missions because the astronauts go to space with an important job, or mission, to do.

These astronauts are getting ready for a mission to fix a telescope that is circling high above Earth. They practice in a giant swimming pool. Using tools underwater gives them an idea of what it will be like working in zero-gravity.

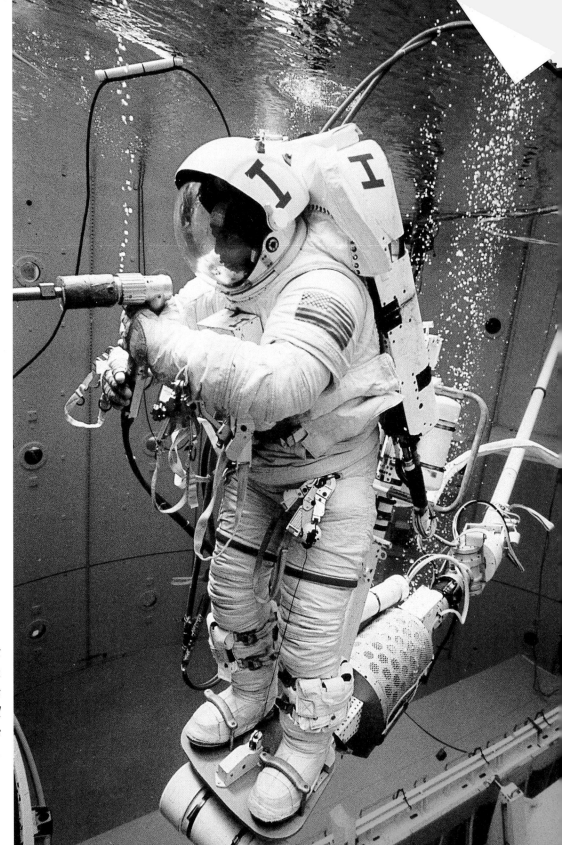

Hooking his feet to a platform helps this astronaut stand still while he drills.

A blast from the booster rockets sends the shuttle Atlantis *soaring toward space.*

The crew heads for the launch pad. Up to seven astronauts fly on each shuttle mission.

Launch day at last. The astronauts board the shuttle and strap themselves in. Three-two-one-zero. Lift-off!

Like a stack of fireworks, the shuttle roars from the launch pad. The astronauts get a bone-rattling ride. They shake up and down. They are pushed back hard as the shuttle fights the pull of gravity.

Suddenly the two booster rockets fall off. Soon the engines stop, and the orange fuel tank beneath the shuttle's belly drops away. Undoing their straps, the astronauts float from their seats. Just eight minutes after launch, they are in space.

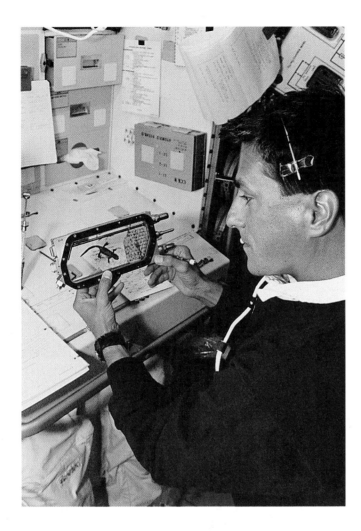

A space-traveling newt helps this astronaut find out how zero-gravity affects animals.

The shuttle begins to orbit, or circle around, Earth. The astronauts get to work. What is the mission this time? To perform science experiments. Many experiments can only be done in the zero-gravity of space. And many products that are hard to make on Earth come out perfect in zero-G.

The astronauts study ways to make superstrong metals and new medicines. They do experiments to find out what happens to plants, animals, and people in space.

To study how people's bodies change in zero-G, astronauts use special equipment like this moving chair.

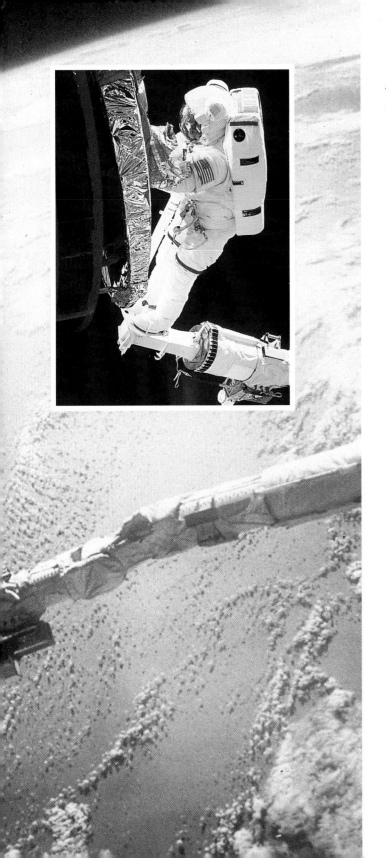

A robot arm helps space workers repair a broken satellite.

On some missions, the shuttle's job is to put a satellite into space. The satellite rides in the long middle part of the spaceship, called the payload bay. The astronauts use a robot arm to pluck the satellite from the bay and send it into orbit around Earth.

If you were an astronaut, you might have to repair an orbiting satellite. You bundle up in your space suit and step out into . . . *nothing*. Your jet backpack lets you fly through black empty space and grab the broken satellite.

Do you like to take photographs? The view from nearly two hundred miles up is awesome. Through the shuttle's windows, you could snap pictures of a whole city, state . . . even a whole country. Photos taken by astronauts help scientists keep an eye on the world's crops, weather, and pollution.

You've got to be quick to photograph Earth. The shuttle travels five miles every second. At that speed, you could aim your camera at a spring-green forest and end up filming wintry mountains on the other side of the world instead.

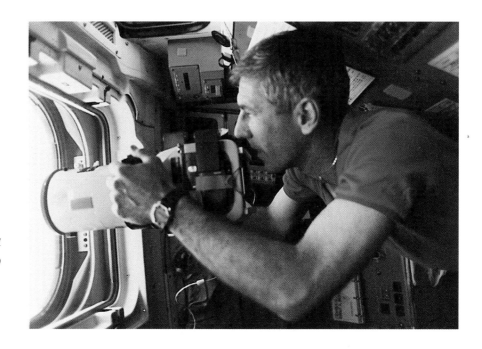

Pictures taken through a shuttle window will help scientists measure this hurricane's size and speed.

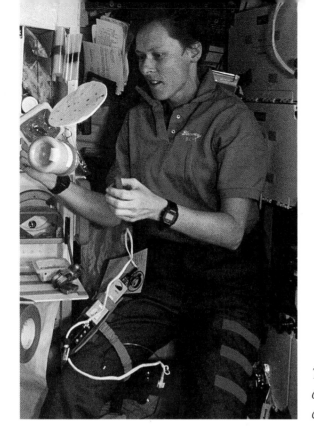

This astronaut is aiming his straw at a blob of juice that has escaped from his drink pouch.

Tortillas and cheese make a tasty snack—if you can catch them!

Imagine eating your regular dinner in zero-gravity. The food, plates, and forks would float around the room! For less mess, shuttle astronauts eat dried food in plastic pouches. They squirt water into the pouches and snap them into a tray. The food sticks to the spoon. Between bites, the spoon sticks to magnetic strips on the tray.

What about snacks? For a treat, astronauts might munch on tortillas, cookies, or M&Ms.

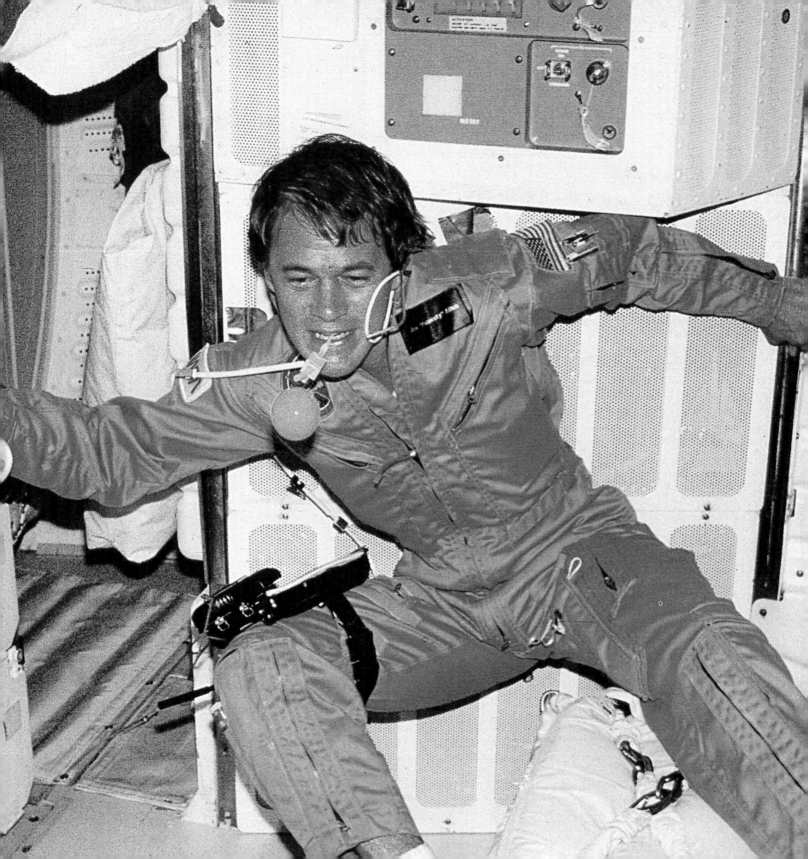

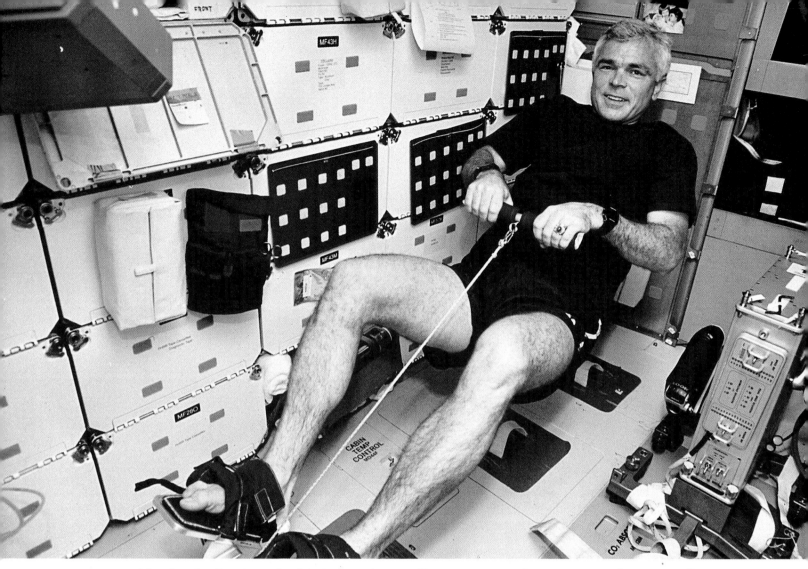

Muscles don't get much of a workout in zero-G, so space travelers must exercise to stay fit.

Many other things that are easy to do on Earth are tricky in zero-gravity. To take a "bath," shuttle astronauts must use two wet towels—one to soap up and one to wipe clean. When they brush their teeth, they have to swallow the toothpaste or spit it into a washcloth.

For a short break, astronauts just fold their arms, stretch out, and rest. At bedtime, they zip themselves into sleeping bags and hook the bags to a wall. That way, they won't bump into anything as they float away with their dreams.

These napping astronauts have different ideas of up and down.

After a week in space, it's time to come home. With a blast from its engines, the shuttle falls from orbit. As gravity grabs the spaceship, the astronauts feel as if they've suddenly gained a few hundred pounds.

Falling to Earth is a wild ride. Air roars past the shuttle, slowing it down and heating it up. Special tiles protect the spaceship from the broiling heat.

The ground rushes into sight. The shuttle glides to the runway. Its wheels touch down, and the astronauts' friends and families cheer.

Mission complete!

As the shuttle nears Earth, it flies without engine power, like a giant glider.

Space campers work at a simulated mission control center. During real space flights, people at mission control talk to the astronauts to help them do their jobs.

Have you ever dreamed of exploring space? These young people are visiting a space camp to find out what it takes to be an astronaut. At camp, they try on space suits and eat space food. Using simulators, they practice flying the shuttle and walking in zero-G.

Space camp students learn that astronauts must be healthy and in good shape. They also need a good education, especially in science and math.

Are you ready to join the astronaut team? Will your dreams come true on a spaceship headed for the stars?

Other simulators give students the sensation of walking in space.

ASTRONAUTS IN TIME

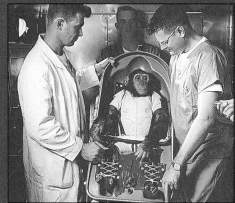

In 1957, Laika the dog became the first earthling in space, traveling in the Russian satellite *Sputnik 2*. Early American "astronauts" included monkeys and chimpanzees.

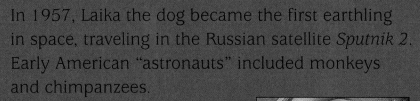

Russians and Americans raced to launch the first person into space. In 1961, the Russians won the race, when Yuri Gagarin circled the world in *Vostok 1*.

The next giant step in the space race came in 1969, when American *Apollo 11* astronauts Neil Armstrong and Edwin "Buzz" Aldrin became the first men on the moon. If you look closely at Aldrin's helmet, you'll see a reflection of Armstrong and the astronauts' landing craft.

Until the first space shuttle took off in 1981, astronauts rode in a tiny black capsule perched on the tip of a giant rocket, like this one. These early spaceships could fly only once. The shuttle and its rocket boosters can be used again and again.

Space travel has always held dangers. The worst accident happened in 1986, when the space shuttle *Challenger* exploded. All seven crew members were killed.

Today the United States is working with other countries to plan an international space station—a high-flying science lab where astronauts from all over the world can live and work for months at a time.

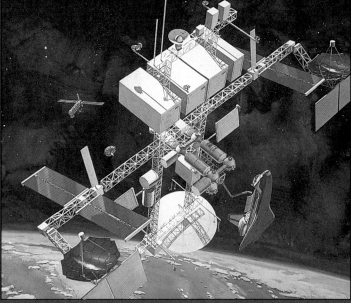

AN ASTRONAUT'S CLOTHING AND EQUIPMENT

During take-off and landing, shuttle astronauts wear **launch/entry suits (LES)**. These ninety-pound space suits protect them from changes in temperature and gravity.

Astronauts wear **extra-vehicular activity (EVA) space suits** when they walk in space. These suits protect them from the Sun's rays and from space dust and rocks. Each EVA space suit has heating and cooling, a microphone and earphones . . . even a juice dispenser.

The **manned maneuvering unit (MMU)** snaps onto the EVA space suit. This jet backpack lets astronauts fly around outside the spaceship.

WORDS TO KNOW

gravity The invisible force that pulls objects toward Earth.

NASA (National Aeronautics and Space Administration) The part of the United States government that runs the space program and plans space missions.

orbit To fly in a circle around Earth or another heavenly body.

payload bay The long middle section of the shuttle, used to carry satellites, space probes, and other equipment into space.

satellite An object that scientists have put into orbit around Earth. Satellites send television programs and telephone calls around the world, collect information on weather and crops, and do many other useful jobs in space.

simulator A full-size model built to look exactly like a machine such as a spaceship, so people can learn how to use the real thing.

space station A large laboratory orbiting Earth, where astronauts can live and work.

Record Breaker

Astronaut Shannon Lucid has spent more time in space than any other American. In 1996, she lived for 188 days on the Russian space station Mir.

Benchmark Books
Marshall Cavendish Corporation
99 White Plains Road
Tarrytown, New York 10591

Library of Congress Cataloging-in-Publication Data
Schomp, Virginia, date.
If you were an—astronaut / Virginia Schomp.
p.   cm.   Includes index.
Summary: Describes the training and experience of astronauts who fly the space shuttle.
!SBN 0-7614-0618-2 (lib. bdg.)
1. Astronautics—Juvenile literature. 2. Astronauts—Juvenile literature. [1. Astronauts. 2. Occupations.] I. Title. II. Title: Astronaut.
TL793.S325   1998   629.45'009—DC21   96-37787   CIP   AC

Photo research by Debbie Needleman

Front cover: *NASA/Photri, Inc.*

The photographs in this book are used by permission and through the courtesy of: *NASA/Photri, Inc.*: 1, 4-5, 6, 8-9, 12, 19, 24, 28 (top right), 29 (top left, bottom right), 30 (top right, bottom right). *The Image Bank*: Michael Melford, 2. *NASA*: 7, 18, 20, 20-21, 23, 25, 30 (left). *NASA/Science Photo Library/Photo Researchers*: 10, 11, 14, 15, 22. *Corbis-Bettmann*: 13, 28 (bottom left), 29 (top right). *NASA/Science Source/Photo Researchers*: 16-17, 17 (inset). *U.S. Space Camp*: Bob Gathany, 26, 27 (left). *Richard Nowitz/Photri, Inc.*: 27 (right). *Sovfoto/Eastfoto*: 28 (top center, bottom right). *NASA and Russian Space Agency/Photri, Inc.*: 31.

Printed in the United States of America
3   5   7   8   6   4   2

INDEX